AF373326

Contents

Introduction

I AWOKE ON 4TH JULY 2017 to realise that I had now lived in my adopted country of South Africa for twenty years to the day. I had moved to Durban, on the east coast, shortly after getting married to my South African boyfriend, who I had met when we were both living in Cambridge, England. He'd been studying when we met and had investigated various options that would enable him to stay in England, or at the very least, Europe. However, nothing came of any of them. Meanwhile, an old family friend back in South Africa had said there was the possibility of a trainee position as a chemical engineer in the sugar company where he was part of the senior management.

As is so often with both proverbial bad pennies and the good things of God, the offer kept coming back to Craig; each time he applied or went for an interview elsewhere and was unsuccessful, this option remained in the background. Eventually, we both reached the conclusion that every other door was going to continue closing until this really was the only one left open.

Craig took the job and headed back to South Africa to get stuck in. In the meantime, I remained at home where a wedding needed to be arranged.

Two weeks after our wedding on 14 June 1997, we found ourselves at London Gatwick airport ready to start the adventure of a lifetime. In my hand, I clutched my blue passport (as it was back then), the name Anna McNally unceremoniously crossed out and Anna Jensen written in its place.

Twenty years later and here I still am. I now have a pink passport and a green South African ID book. And I think it is the possession of both those two official identification documents that sums up expat living; I'm neither one thing nor the other but am sort of both.

Several years ago, I felt God challenge me on this. I was living here in South Africa and yet still called England 'back home'. Somehow that didn't seem quite the way God intended it to be. And then I read this prophetic picture in the book of Ezekiel,

'A great eagle with great wings and long pinions, rich in plumage of many colors, came to Lebanon and took the top of the cedar. 4 He broke off the topmost of its young twigs and carried it to a land of trade and set it in a city of merchants. 5 Then he took of the seed of the land and planted it in fertile soil. He placed it beside abundant waters. He set it like a willow twig, 6 and it sprouted and became a low spreading vine, and its branches turned toward him, and its roots remained where it stood. So it became a vine and produced branches and put out boughs.' Ezekiel 17:3-6

I was immediately convicted. Although England is the place of my birth and upbringing, I have been 'plucked' and purposefully brought to South Africa where I 'live and breathe and have my being'. Paul here assures us that God has 'determined allotted periods and the boundaries of [our] dwelling place' (Acts 17:26-28). I do not live where I do because of the person I've married or the job he has; I live here because God has chosen this to be the place where I will flourish and grow, where my roots will be well watered and deep.

As I allowed this to settle in my heart, my living here became equally more settled. I no longer hankered for ' back home' as I pursued living 'at home' here.

Now, this isn't to say I have become South African. That will never be the case, no matter how long I live here or how settled I am. Some of the fundamentals which make me who I am are there because I was brought up in a different country to this one. Equally, however, when I return on holiday to the UK, I realise I am no longer as fully English as I was. I am, for example, an entirely South African parent (I hear myself wonder how my sister copes with her kids in the winter when it's cold and dark and raining). I don't quite fit in either place, I have the pink passport and the green ID book. But I'm not really supposed to. My citizenship is in Heaven, and it is only there that I will ever be fully 'home'.

I now enjoy the best of both countries and cultures, finding humour in our difference and comfort in our similarity. So much so that I decided it might be fun to share some of my stories from those early days. And so 'Twenty Years an Ex-Pat' was born; a blog, now little book, that tells some of the more amusing tales of settling in. I trust you will enjoy this short collection of thoughts and memories.

1

Independence Day

For I know the plans I have for you, declares the LORD, plans for

welfare and not for evil, to give you a future and a hope

Jeremiah 29:11

FRIDAY 4TH JULY 1997 - my personal Independence Day. Not from the

tyranny of a British Crown but rather from my life of familiarity and

comfort. Twenty years ago today I arrived on South African soil with

my two-week-old husband (yes, that anniversary has just been

celebrated too), bound for a town 170km north of Durban which

even most of his mates hadn't ever visited - or felt the need to -

much less lived there.

Empangeni, home of the Tongaat-Hulett sugar mill at Felixton

where Craig had been training as an apprentice process engineer since earlier in the year. Empangeni - Afrikaans, hot, dusty and distant.

We arrived at the then Louis Botha airport in Durban at about lunchtime after leaving London Gatwick the night before. Now that's a memory I shan't forget - saying goodbye to my mum and dad for I wasn't sure how long for, following Craig's family (who had been over for the wedding and who happened to be booked on the same flight home) as they disappeared down the blue-walled and - carpeted departure tunnel from where we would be ushered onto a plane that would take me from all I knew as familiar. The excitement of getting married, of being on honeymoon, of going with my man to new places and new adventures was distinctly dulled by the tears of farewell that afternoon.

But to Durban. We were collected from the airport and taken to Craig's family home on the other side of Durban where our worldly belongings, impossibly packed into an aging white VW kombi, awaited our arrival for their relocation. I think we probably had a quick cup of tea (as essential a liquid in South Africa as it is ever hailed in England) and maybe a sandwich and then we were off.

Piled, or perhaps more accurately, squeezed into the kombi, the new Mr. and Mrs. Jensen bid another farewell, albeit for a shorter time and distance, and began the two-hour drive up the coast to our City of Dreams.

The drive from Durban to Empangeni is still one of the most indelibly seared memories in my psyche. The July light, a beautiful, dusty yellow at this time of year; the green humps of the sugar cane fields; a beguiling, sparkling blue Indian Ocean; and a twisting sweep of deserted freeway leading to I knew not what. Excited to finally be on our own, thrilled at the landscape through which we traveled, alive with the new ideas and possibilities ahead. And intensely, bubblingly, sickeningly nervous. My Independence Day.

Touchdown!

Touchdown!

Of

Brown oval leather

On

Muddied, churned up turf

To the sound of roars and cheers

No

Of

Black round rubber

On

Heated, hardened tarmac

To the silent, inward tears of insecurity and excitement

'Ladies and gentlemen

    We have arrived at our destination

    Please remain seated until we have come to a complete

        Stop'

While I wait to

    Start

My journey, my adventure

My own personal romance

My 'Out of Africa'

New bride

New place

New life

New me?

Prayer

Lord, thank you that you have plans that are to prosper and not to harm me. Thank you that you will bring them into being at the right time and in the right way.

Help me to trust you when the changes seem too big for me to handle, too scary for me to cope with.

2
Where Were You?

Are not two sparrows sold for a penny? And not one of them will fall to the ground apart from your Father. But even the hairs of your head are all numbered. Fear not, therefore; you are of more value than many sparrows

Matthew 10:29-31

[This was a post originally written on around 31 August 2017, the twentieth anniversary of the death of Diana, Princess of Wales. The newspaper headlines were full of reminders of that fateful day, and I got to reminiscing about what Craig and I had been doing at the time.]

For a certain generation, the query would be- 'where were you when Elvis died?' or 'when JFK was shot?'. For me and mine -

'Princess Di?'. Whilst the world, or perhaps more accurately the media, take a delve into the minutiae of the reply, I confess to embarking on something of a memory-fest myself.

We are standing in a sun-lit lounge bar, devoid of life except ourselves. An impression of red upholstery and green sugar cane, beer taps expertly polished and the murmur of drinks fridges attesting to their cooled delights. Eventually someone - a lady? A man? I really can't remember - appears. No greeting of warm welcome, no apology at having abandoned their station of succour. Just 'Lady Di is dead'. In hushed tones of awed excitement. Pardon??!

To fully comprehend our intense bewilderment, it is necessary to take several turns of dirt road backward.

It was our first weekend away. Craig had finished early and was all set to take his wife on a true African bush adventure. He'd asked around and found the perfect spot to visit -a small game park about an hour or so further north where you sleep in, wait for it...tree houses! Groovy cool, I thought.

We piled ourselves and a couple of bags into our new-to-us dark blue Toyota Cressida (the Kombi, with its headlight that needed banging at every set of traffic lights to ensure it was still alight, had been happily reunited with its owners back in Durban, having performed its role as beast of burden admirably) and headed up the freeway. We drove for about an hour on a road that, back then, boasted little traffic, other than trucks carrying sugar cane or logs to their respective processing sites, and 4x4 pickups laden with fishing-trippers or farmers and their vegetables. We passed fields of thick-stalked, fibre-rich sugar cane and row upon row of blue gums, practising their future role as telegraph poles with epileptic-inducing, evening-sun-flashes of regularity.

Eventually, we turned off and found the tar giving way to dust and dirt and small boulders. Continuing further, we located the entrance to our weekend retreat, passing a cheetah sanctuary and authentic Zulu cultural village along the way. We collected our key from the reception desk, which looked remarkably non-treehouse or African bush-like, and were pointed in the general direction of our own personal tree, to which we dutifully (apprehensively?) proceeded.

This particular game park, at that time anyway, was a haven for buck and birds, as opposed to lion or leopard. A sleepy hush hung in the air, with the days' warmth resting gently between the thorn bushes where we spied impala and nyala browsing their way through supper. Our tires cracked and rolled their way through fallen twigs, leaves and miniature sand dunes. Round a couple of corners and we found our tree!

It was a large, sturdy-looking specimen, not unlike the Faraway

Tree of childhood storytime. It didn't, however, boast a helter-skelter slide or circular lift. Just some rickety stairs leading to a platform with some metal chairs and a table, and a sort of wooden tent affair which was the bedroom. Below the stairs was a, very rustic (no, not English quaint rustic; proper, 'Golly, how will we eat?' rustic), kitchen area and a toilet/shower area. All the windows were covered with a fine mesh and outer layer of chicken wire. Most unexplainable to this fair maid from gentler shores; less so to the more experienced African wanderer that sits here today!

We unpacked our bits and bobs, tried to make something of the kitchen, avoided the toilet for as long as humanly possible and then ascended into the foliage for a drink and a relax.

Only to observe that the twig behind Craig's shoulder wasn't, in fact, a twig at all, but rather a small but inquisitive tree snake making its way purposefully towards Craig's shoulder and ultimately his eminently nibbleable ear. Coolly and calmly (ha, ha) we clattered back down the stairs and decided a trip in the car back to reception, where there would no doubt be a snake-identifier chart thing, was most assuredly in order. In we went, nonchalantly trying not to look every inch the scared townies that we were and attempted to reassure ourselves that our weekend wasn't over before it began. It was at this time that we heard the story of the German tourist who was reliably informed that an iguana is a regular and harmless fixture of every lodge in the game park. But that's for another day ...

Suitably placated, we returned to our lofty abode to once more embark on our relaxing weekend away. No snakes this time. Very pleasant, just the sound of the insects buzzing softly around us.

Oh, and therein lay my ruin. Flappy Things. September in Empangeni and further north is a few degrees warmer than Durban and, as such, Flappy Things hatch and come out to play awhile earlier. The helpful Tripadvisors Craig had consulted had neglected to inform him about the Flappy Things that inhabit tree houses just then. Moths attracted to every lumen they could find; wasps with long dangly bodies and wobbly feelers eager to taste whatever delights they could find; whining mosquitoes playing bedtime hide and seek - you can hear them in the dark but you can never find them when the light's on; little brown Christmas beetles, round bodies completely inappropriate for their function of flight; and flying ants, one minute taking to the skies on their see-through double wings, the next plopping to the ground in a brown wriggly earth bound creep.

I'm sure we had a great weekend away. We were able to walk amongst the thorn trees and see how close to the animals we could get (not very), our tree was visited by warthog and zebra every couple of hours, we even found a swimming pool to relax beside. But my abiding memory will always be of Flappy Things.

And that brings me back to 'Lady Di is dead'. A weekend of trees and snakes and Flappy Things and bush left us completely unprepared for the reimersion into a less than perfect reality that was that pronouncement. Suddenly we were thrust back into the world of celebrities and their watchers, of power-struggles and politics, of national grief, whether real or imagined, and, ultimately, the truth that life isn't as certain as we like to think it.

Perhaps escape and immersion into that other world of Flappy Things and the gloriously uncomfortable is, in fact, a salve for our souls, a brief encounter with the primitive, whispering that our sophistication is not nearly so refreshing or replenishing as we hold it to be. And perhaps the neon-lit events of world-stage history serve as beacons in whose light our own unnoticed stories glow a little brighter.

Where were you?

Flappy Things

There are lots of insects in Africa
      Of really quite high calibre.
To me, their name is Flappy Things
      Because they sport such bugly wings.

They thump, they bump
      they float, they fly;
        this mainly when the day is nigh.
Quite blind, I'm sure, to all around
      'Cept me,
        Whom they seem to hound.

I wonder why an ant should rise
    above its earthbound creep and crawl?
      Or why a beetle tries at all
        when fashioned like a ball?

'All creatures great and small
The Lord God made them all'
  Was this for me
      That I might see

His humour and His fun?

For what other than these Flappy Things
        could carry so much mirth
That when I think of other times
        a chuckle they will birth?

Prayer

Father, I worship you as the Maker of the Universe, from the stars in the sky to the insects and flowers in my garden. Thank you that you know and care for each one.

Thank you that you also know me. You count the hairs on my head, you know my coming and my going, you know each of my thoughts. Help me to rest in your love for me during this time, even as I try to help others know they are also much loved.

3

The Great Unpack or Treasures Rediscovered

...forgetting what lies behind and straining forward to what lies

ahead...

Philippians 3:13

AFTER A ROMANTIC NIGHT spent on a mattress on the somewhat coldly-tiled floor of our new home, our attention turned to that overstuffed white combi currently resting from the previous day's exertions in our little garage-without-a-door. Our newly-purchased, very purple, bed was still unhelpfully located at the bottom of a pile of Fraser's International Movers' brown cardboard boxes and so, should we prefer a more dignified end to our day than our start, we were going to have to get moving, as it were.

Truth to tell, I was quite looking forward to the upcoming project. The packing had been undertaken some months previously from my little flat in Cambridge, without Craig's presence as he'd already long left the country. I'd arranged a moving company; determined that all our worldly goods would actually quite easily utilise only half a container; had arranged for boxes to be dropped off at said little flat; and then proceeded to fold my way through numerous copies of the Cambridge Evening News in some effort at preserving our meagre array of material wealth. Seeing as much water had flowed under the bridge of time - small matters, like arranging a wedding, getting married, going on honeymoon, sitting a PhD *viva* (Craig, not me!) and travelling to the other side of the world - I really wasn't too sure what exactly was contained within these humble-seeming treasure chests.

And so, hey ho, off to work we go. We shoved and lugged and pushed and carried our way through the combi's cargo until finally, everything had found its place somewhere in the house. The purple bed was manoeuvred up the angled stairway and given pride of place in our uncurtained, un-rugged bedroom. The unprepossessing boxes of delights awaited our attention in the lounge. We were ready for discovery.

I suspect we stopped for a cup of tea at this point.

Ripping off the brown, frustratingly sticky parcel tape from the first box, we delved inside to see what I may have meant by the large, black-felt tipped label 'KITCHEN'. Sheets of Cambridge Evening News were soon scattered around the lounge, in a giant-sized parody of the confetti used only two weeks previously. We gleefully exclaimed our delight at the reuniting of ourselves with the blue plastic colander and the little wooden chopping board, so essential to our 'Boys' Food' of sausage pasta; the CD's and stereo when we moved on to 'LOUNGE'; Craig's ornamental rowing blade awarded on a race victory and not sawn in half as I'd told him when describing the dilemma the shipping company had had when they came to collect it.

Twenty years on I can't remember all that we unpacked that weekend or continued to unpack and sort over the next couple of weeks. But I am struck by the remembrance of the little and yet important items I'd stowed away for their sea-faring adventure, for the value I'd chosen to invest in those things which to others were meaningless. Did I really think it would be impossible to buy a blue plastic colander in South Africa? Or was I, on some level, trying to preserve and hold onto that which was familiar, safe, known, as I prepared for the external revolution of marriage and move to another hemisphere?

The wooden chopping board was finally, somewhat sadly,

deposited in our dustbin just about a month ago, cracked and mouldy from overuse. I confess to a pull on my heartstrings as I helped it on its final journey to the local dump. The blue plastic colander has given way to a shiny new metal one. We do still have the little teaspoon, pilfered from the Trinity College Kitchens (!)now lurking unused in an overstuffed drawer. And yes, the rowing blade still adorns our wall.

Unpacking

Unpacking

Heaving, pushing

    Pulling, shoving

Ripping, tearing

    Now discovering

Pieces wrapped in white and black

 Re-found, as though amnesiac,

    we delightedly exclaim.

So carefully I stored those treasures

Safely packing all that mattered

Bringing all I knew so well

A safety net of sorts to use

    When tumbling

        falling

            into strange

 Would all become too much.

The hippo mug I'd had for years

The backpack hauled to south and east

The books and music, files and folders

Reminders of another time.

Even now I stop to think

Did I really bring such trinkets

    of insignificance?

Had I bestowed a value

    where worth should not have been

And left unloved

             unwrapped

                unseen

                    a pearl of priceless portion?

This leads me on to serious thought

That on this longer Journey

      Life

Am I packing what I ought?

Do I stow a grudge from you

    But leave back a smile or few?

Do I hold what made me cry

    While laughter I let fall and die

Father, during this season of uncertainty and change, thank you that you have a plan and a purpose in mind, both for me and the whole of humanity. Please help me to correctly assess what is important and should be carried with me, and what should be left behind. Help me to keep my eyes fixed on Jesus throughout this time.

4
Birthdays

A new commandment I give to you, that you love one another: just as I have loved you, you also are to love one another. By this all people will know that you are my disciples, if you have love for one another.

John 13:34-35

IT'S A FUNNY THING, but where I have many detailed memories of much of the early years here in South Africa, the October month of birthdays seems to have been left out of my recollections! I'm not sure if that means they were so awful that I've blocked them out completely or simply that they were rather mundane and lacklustre. I suspect the latter! I'm sure they were special and enjoyable at the time, they just don't seem to have made much of an impression.

When we first moved to Empangeni we lived in a small complex in a quiet road just behind the shopping centre. I could walk to Pick n Pay (pronounced something like Puck n Pie by the locals - took a while to not giggle) and lug back my shopping bags, just like the old days in Cambridge, although not on a bicycle. That mode of transport is reserved for whizzing round every available street in any given city vying to be the first to complete the prescribed course whilst wearing suitably 'Tour de France' outfits, or racing ludicrously long distances between locations all before lunchtime. Shopping bags on handlebars? No.

Our complex was also near the local cemetery, which conveniently enough was overlooked by the local nursing home for the elderly...

At the end of our quiet road were the Post Boxes; blue metal stacks of little boxes with little keyholes, into one of which we would insert our little key in order to reveal the untold hidden delights of International Post. Each day, I took myself for a meander down our road with the express purpose of treasure-seeking. The road was a loop, so I walked down the one side which followed the fence of a field on the left and dog-guarded houses on the right. How I hoped the gates were all securely closed to the barking, snarling, yapping inhabitants of those homes. Once I reached the Post Boxes, I would take my silver talisman, find the door with my number on it and release the lock. Then, peering in, I'd look for the post. Blue folded airmail letters, with their red markings down the side, were always the best to discover - they were the link with the familiar that I was looking for. An empty dark loneliness was the worst to find; that reminded me I was far from all that had been normal and now had to get on with this new. Still, tomorrow was always another day …

The boxes stood on a patch of untended ground, a place where the grass grew brown over the winter, where the birds could be heard over the conversations of the dogs behind me and where it was actually quite pleasant to linger and gaze at the surrounding fields before heading back the other side of the loop and home. On a good day, I would flap my blue envelope as I walked, savouring the reading of it until I got home to the lounge and a cup of tea. On a not so good day, I would think of what else I should do now that distraction was completed. This side of the loop had houses on both sides - more dogs to avoid but more to captivate my attention perhaps.

I do remember receiving birthday cards in my box of postal delights that first year. The first birthday I have the clearest recollection of was from a few years later though. Craig's sister, Lana, had moved into her own place in the north Durban suburbs. We'd become friends when she was living in Cambridge - in fact, I was friends with her before I was 'friends' with her brother - and had continued the friendship once we'd also become family.

This particular year, and I can't say I remember which one it was exactly, she'd invited us to her new spot for tea. We arrived late and I was in the foulest of moods following a bit of aggro with another friend earlier in the day. We arrived and stopped in the black-gated entrance to her complex. I climbed out of the car and buzzed the intercom, announcing grumpily and unceremoniously that we had arrived, that I'd had a miserable day and I just wanted to go home. Lana, to her credit, opened the gate to let us in and didn't throw the surprise birthday dinner all over me! She'd cooked my favourite of the time, Tex-Mex, and invited a couple of other mutual friends over to celebrate with us.

And I think therein lies the reason why those early birthdays lay somewhat forgotten, whilst others shine through so clearly - it's not the passage of time that makes the difference, it's the connectivity with others, the history that's been created and contemplated and cackled over that makes them so special. Lana knew what meal I liked; she knew which friends I would enjoy having around. She knew my story.

And that's what we celebrate, after all - a collective memory of years gone before, of a life lived alongside each other and the beckoning of a future we can wander into together.

Happy Birthday!

Birthday poem

Are birthdays

    all cake and candles?

        Presents and parties?

Or are they community caring

    Who sing -

        in tune or out -

And laugh and live

    as pieces of the puzzle

        that I have become.

Who reminisce and revisit

    who revive

        And who remind me

        To be real

Prayer

Father, thank you that have placed me in community, amongst people who love me and who I can also love. Help me to find ways to show this love, especially as we navigate through difficult times together.

5
Christmas in 'July'

Again Jesus spoke to them, saying, "I am the light of the world.

Whoever follows me will not walk in darkness, but will have the light

of life.

John 8:12

I'M NOT SURE I WILL ever get used to hot Christmases. Even after 20 years, I simply can't do it. By around October (birthday month, I suppose) my mind has started to imagine golden leaves falling into scrunchy heaps from the trees, steamy breath lingering in the mornings and evenings and red noses, frozen chins, puckered cheeks. I think fairy lights, candles, hot chocolate, and weighty desserts.

But all around me calls the lie to these many anticipations. Instead, the days are getting longer - surely they should be shorter by now? When it rains, as it now starts to do, it's not accompanied by chilblains and blisters but headache-inducing humidity which I'd forgotten I suffer from. And then, when standing in my shorts and T-shirt at the supermarket checkout counter, waiting to pay for my giant watermelon and newly in-season mangoes, I'm regaled with crooning dreams of white Christmases, and the disconnect is notched up to the ridiculous.

It's not that I don't love summer in Durban. I truly do. I love being hot and seeing the sunshine every day, I love the (slightly) increased hours of daylight and the fact that I don't need piles of clothes, just in case it turns chilly. It's just it doesn't fit with Christmas. I still get confused about Easter too - that's a springtime festival, associated with daffodils and warmer days, not autumn. And spring day is September 1st? It all makes me feel like I'm living upside down.

My first experience of a hot Christmas also involved my folks, who had come over to visit us for the first time since we'd moved to SA in that July. It was so special having them here, and I was super keen to show them all that I'd discovered about my new home. At the time, we were living in a small flat above the maintenance workshop at the factory where Craig worked, about 2 hours' drive north of Durban. Sleeping for the first couple of nights on a ludicrously low and awfully solid futon in our lounge, they were woken each morning at about 4.00am by the family of mina birds nesting in the broken air-conditioning unit which protruded through the wall. Many and varied were the attempts to relocate said family from their chosen abode over the next couple of days, with pretty limited success. Their next early wake-up came from the hadeda ibis who start their day with screeches of epic proportions. To give those not initiated in their song an idea - my kids joke that they are the only birds scared of heights, as they scream with fear as they fly overhead! It is not a gentle start to anyone's morning, let alone someone sleeping on a Flintstone mattress and already woken by the mina neighbours.

After the first couple of days spent at home, with my folks chuckling at Craig as he walked down to work in his shorts and long socks (thankfully the work outfit has matured to long trousers, rather than socks), we climbed into our new-to-us Toyota Cressida and commenced an eventful journey to the Kruger National Park. Given we had a drive of over 600km (370 miles) ahead of us, it was a little disconcerting when the radiator began to overheat whilst traversing the first serious hill a mere 100 km from home. In hindsight, we should probably have returned from whence we came, fixed the car and started again. But who lives by hindsight? We continued, stopping at frustratingly frequent intervals to check and add more water. That said, it was a beautiful journey. We drove alongside fields of thick-stalked, lush green sugar cane, through forests of darker green gum trees, past dams too big to see across, climbing hills and viewing valleys of colours and proportions my folks and I were in awe of. Every now and then we would come across an individual, or a small group of people, walking on the road's edge, seemingly travelling from nowhere to nowhere; this latter provided us with many hours of contemplation as we pondered the reality of life for a genuinely rural population.

Hailing as I do from an overpopulated island in the Northern Hemisphere, this driving under a wide-open sky, with landscapes tinged purple through distance, ignited a love for road trips that lives me with still.

I digress; lest we forget we are discussing the peculiarity of Christmas in the summer, it was hot. And sunny. And hot. Just hot. We were really hot. Even the car was hot. Steaming hot!

We eventually arrived at our accommodation just outside Kruger Park (after being told we couldn't picnic in a certain spot on the way because of murderous bandits roaming the area!) and opted for an early night as we intended to be up at near-dawn in order to get to the park as the gates were opening.

Early we rose; early we didn't get to the park. Our poor overworked, overheated radiator gave up halfway there, leaving streams in the wasteland of our surrounds and us having to call for back-up from the closest garage. A one-armed mechanic (I kid you not) came to our rescue and spent the rest of the day replacing the radiator while we lounged restlessly back at our accommodation. A great day of game-spotting wasn't had by all.

We tried again the next day. Up we got, with eager anticipation for the day ahead, knowing our steed would today be trusty. We drove through those park gates confident of the crush of elephants, buffalo, lions that awaited us. We drove for three hours and saw nothing. Absolutely nothing. Not a bird, not an insect. Nothing. Then we saw a tortoise. Never has the little shelled creature experienced such effusive delight at its diminutive presence. Success! We did then come across two cheetahs lying in the road just around the corner. Alas, poor tortoise, your prowess was short-lived.

After a wonderful trip exploring Kruger Park, God's Window, Pilgrim's Rest and other northerly locales we drove (uneventfully) back to Durban, met my sister who had flown over for the holidays, climbed aboard another plane and made our way to Cape Town. We spent a few days in and around Cape Town, visited some wine farms, popped into a couple of museums that displayed farming implements still used by my grandad back home then took our little white hire car up the Garden Route to Knysna and Plettenberg Bay before catching a flight out of East London and so to Christmas.

I think there are possibly two differences between a hot and cold Christmas Day that are most evident. First, what to wear? The traditional 'purchased especially' super smart, super warm Christmas outfit doesn't quite work when all you actually want to do is plop into a nearby swimming pool to cool off. And secondly, the food. Christmas is turkey, cranberry sauce, stuffing balls, brussels sprouts followed by Christmas pudding and custard, warm mince pies and copious quantities of festive chocolate. Oh, and warm mulled wine. It's also about cold, windy walks to build up an appetite worthy of such a spread - wellies, hats, scarves, and gloves. It just isn't cold meats and salad followed by a fight for the best position under the ceiling fan.

Over the years I've tried to acclimatise to, accommodate, embrace even, these differences, tried to overcome the homesickness that reappears every December as I remember what it 'should' be like at Christmas. And I've come to a conclusion. So long as I think of it as the best kind of family summer holiday rather than a cosy Christmas celebration then I have a ball, I love it. Perhaps this is how it should be - perhaps a move to the other side of the world is the best way to evaluate a truth that I've somehow lost along the way. What, after all, is Christmas? What, really, is the 'reason for the season', whether it be summer or winter?

'Tis the season

'Tis The Season

'Tis the season to be jolly

   To light the candles

      Draw the curtains

         Be warm

            Be cosy

               Be a little

                  self-indulgent

Time to buy the turkey

   Check the cake

      (baked in August)

   Write the lists

      And choose the gifts

Time to scare the dark away

   With trees and twinkles

      And lighted fairies

         dancing in the houses

           of windows I pass

But here it's just too hot for that

For here the time has changed

    To poolside days

        and sun-burnt nights

    To litchis, grapes and mangoes

So, I sadly sigh,

    this Christmas isn't Christmas

    and the season sits all wrong

But surely

    'Tis still the season to be jolly?

    When Him from heaven gifted earth

        The hot, the cold, the in-between

    The loved, the well connected,

        The happy and the free;

            The lonely and the desperate and the lost.

    The ones that know

            'Immanuel'

    And those that think Him far.

To all, He is the light of life

    the brighter Candle in the dark

        for me to place in prominence

in this window of my heart

That they would pass and see

The Reason for the Season

Prayer

Father, thank you for sending your precious Son, Jesus, into the world. Thank you that he is the light who shines in the darkest places and times. Help me to reflect his light wherever I go.

6

Fireplaces

Splendor and majesty are before him; strength and beauty are in his sanctuary. Psalm 96:6

So HERE WE ARE, a week away from our wedding anniversary, less than a month away from my ex-pat anniversary. I married in summer and travelled to winter.

And it's at this time of year, when it (finally for some) starts to get a little chillier in the mornings, a little darker in the evenings, that I reconnect with a most English love - fire! Ever since being a little girl, I have loved open fires in winter. My grandad always had the biggest, hottest, fiercest fire in his grate whenever we visited him in Norfolk. I loved walking into his lounge to be greeted by the orange glow on the walls, feel the tingle in my warming cheeks. At home, we also had glorious fires, besides which we would listen to the Top 40 on Sunday afternoons while toasting crumpets on a long-handled fork and drinking tea. On Christmas Eve, Dad would do a special stoking of the fire, covering it with fine coal dust before heading for bed; on Christmas Morning, there would still be a soft glow amongst the ashes which, with a gentle blow, could be coaxed back into delightful life.

My first experience of fires and fireplaces in South Africa was a little different. Here, although it was July and technically winter, the fire was used not primarily for warming oneself, but rather for cooking. Cooking meat. Lots of meat.

One afternoon we were invited to Craig's immediate boss' home for a potjie (said _poykie_, English reader friend). To the uninitiated, a potjie is a man's casserole. It's cooked in a big black witch's cauldron of a pot over an open fire, outdoors of course, and is presided over by the men of the party. There is much pride over what is thrown into the pot, with competitions held across the country to find the best recipe. It takes hours and hours to cook all that is thrown into the pot to the right consistency of fall-off-the-bone meat and charred-to-a-crisp potatoes or vegetables. It takes hours and hours of drinking beer and watching rugby to get this just right. It is exclusively men's work.

So, we sat around Craig's boss' fire chatting about this and that.

The time ticked by, we continued to sit around the fire chatting about this and that. And the time ticked by some more. At one point, we discussed cannibalistic options of succour, with Craig declaring there would be no merit to eating his new wife as she is 'full of bone and gristle'. Ladies, never stress again to lose weight for your man. He just thinks of bone and gristle!

By the end of a rather long, but actually quite fun afternoon, we did get to eat a delicious plate of casserole next to a bonfire of an oven. I obviously enjoyed the occasion terrifically, as my 30th birthday party was a joint affair with my sister-in-law where potjie was the primary focus.

The next big fire event was The Mates' Braai (barbecue). We went off to join a few other couples, some recently married, some not yet, for an afternoon of jollity around the fire, taking with us the requisite half a cow to cook (no cardboard burgers or sausages here. And certainly nothing 'beany'). Naively I thought this meant we all sat around the fire having an enjoyable time together, maybe strumming a guitar or something. I soon discovered the error in my thinking when I realised I was the only female standing within warming distance of said fire, whilst all the other gals were sitting comfortably inside, happy to leave their men to deal with the great outdoors. It was really rather comical, as I persisted in my efforts to intelligently discuss the latest efforts of the Springbok scrum-half rather than prepare a glut of salads that no-one would eat. Again, a great time was actually had by all, but the initial culture shock surrounding braai etiquette was quite as fierce as the fires themselves, to begin with.

My favourite 'fire-time' here is when we go camping. I love lighting the fire mid-afternoon where we can sit and relax after what has probably been quite an active day until then. We play musical chairs with the smoke for a while, but once the blaze takes hold, it's magical. The sky mirrors the oranges and reds of the fire as the sun goes down, then the darkness is pierced by a million, trillion stars that are never seen in the city. Crickets start to chirrup and any nearby frogs croak throatily. On a still night with little wind, the breaking and cracking of the logs as they turn slowly to charcoal and then to ash punctuates the murmured conversations between family and friends like a soft lullaby. There is nothing like it.

One Saturday morning, after living in Umdloti for a few years, we were out at the nearby hardware store where they had, of all things, indoor fireplace kits on special. I was so excited - I could have a fire of my own, in my lounge, in my house. We bought one. We came home and Craig proceeded to make holes in the ceiling and roof for the chimney, which poked proudly upward from our newest toy. We bought firelighters and matches and wood. And we lit the fire. We were smoked out in seconds!

We have made considerably more successful fires at home since that first attempt. Craig has a rule that it can only be lit when the outside temperature drops below 20 degrees because otherwise, he will melt into a pool of self-induced sweatiness! Friends are always aghast when I say I have a fireplace at home, laughing at my owning such a thing. Laughing, that is, until the outside temperature drops below 20 degrees and then they all wish they were here. I was delighted to learn, only yesterday, that a friend up the road has a fireplace, and she's from East Germany, so considerably more inured to the cold than I.

What draws us, what draws me, to these mini infernos of flame? Whether we cook on them, sit by them or just warm a space with them, they are mesmerising; a hypnotising world of glowing light and smouldering dark, of dancers and ballads and melodies, of songs that were sung and are still being hummed. It is the safety of childhood giving warmth to today, and the dreams of tomorrow taking shape as we watch.

It is the fire itself the poem we read.

Prayer
Father, thank you that in your presence there is both strength

and beauty. Help me to quieten myself and gaze upon you during this time, drawing closer and loving you more.

7

You Say Tomato ...

There is neither Jew nor Greek, there is neither slave nor free, there

is no male and female, for you are all one in Christ Jesus

Galatians 3:28

RELOCATING HALFWAY ACROSS THE WORLD didn't seem quite so daunting, given I was going to a region that spoke the same language as me. Or so I thought!

I guess I should have been slightly forewarned. Even when I first met Craig, although he was speaking perfectly acceptable English, I do confess to understanding little of the conversations I was engaged in. My occasional 'yes's and 'no's did elicit slightly strange looks from Craig, so I think it's safe to say I was missing the point in many an instance.

Empangeni, our new home town, wasn't the most English of all in KwaZulu-Natal. There is a fair smattering of Afrikaans-speaking people, and as the name of the province would suggest, plenty of Zulu speakers. Thankfully, both parties are very kind and talented and have learned to speak English as their second language, enabling me to be lazy. I say to my shame.

Once we had settled into our little house and Craig had headed back to work, I was left to brave the world of Afrikaans and Zulu English-second language speakers all on my own. My first foray into their world involved grocery shopping.

Over the road from our house was the local shopping mall, replete with supermarkets, a picture-framers, a couple of furniture stores and a very friendly barber-cum-sugar-cane-farmer. Funnily enough, when I lived in Cambridge, I lived over the road from Sainsbury's; and there, quite frankly, the similarity ends.

I took myself off for an outing, in search of ingredients for something I wanted to make that evening. I forget now what it was, but I know it required the purchase of some sort of nuts. Why I remember this particular ingredient will soon become apparent. I wandered over the road and into the mall.

As soon as I walked through the entrance, my nostrils were assailed by the sweet smell of baking. Mr. Biscuit, or Biscuit King - I can't remember whether common or royal - was located just inside the door and did a roaring trade every day in a variety of freshly baked, well, biscuits. Although the smell was enticing, an actual nibble was always a little disappointing so, surprising for me, I wasn't particularly tempted. Pick n Pay ('Puck n Pie', as I have said elsewhere) was my focus, and I was not to be turned.

There were two supermarkets in this shopping mall, at opposite ends of the centre. The one was Shoprite Checkers, a store trading at the cheaper end of the scale. It wasn't my favourite. It was always busy, I could never find anything I was looking for amongst the pallets and piles of stuff that seemed to occupy every aisle. And the checkout didn't have a handy conveyor belt for moving my purchases from my end to the cashier, so it was labour intensive and slow.

Instead, I frequented the considerably more upmarket Pick n Pay. Now, when I say 'upmarket', don't for one instance think I mean Woolworths or Waitrose. I simply mean it had slightly neater shelves and, joy of all joys, a moving conveyor belt at the checkout. The fruit and vegetables were still battered and dusty looking, clearly tired out and disillusioned after sitting, unbought, on shelves day after day. The cheese ranged from the mildest cheddar a child could wish for, through red-skinned rubbery hunks of gouda right to 'Tusser's Loaf', a decidedly odd example of processed milk solids. The cereal aisle was miles and miles of cornflakes, bran flakes, muesli, porridge

- and nothing else. Ready meals were unknown. I despaired.

And so to my quest for nuts and the realisation that whilst English may be the language in play, it wasn't necessarily the same English we were playing with.

I had hunted high and low for the nuts I was looking for and just couldn't find them anywhere. In the end, I decided I was surely grown-up enough to go and ask one of the friendly assistants who could be found throughout the store. I sidled up to one, and asked, very politely, if she could tell me where the nuts could be found. She merely looked at me blankly and said 'What?'. I repeated my question, probably reverting to English Person Abroad stereotype by speaking just a little louder and slower, hoping this would help. As all English People Abroad stereotypes have found to their cost, it didn't.

It should be said at this point, in case it has slipped our minds, that I come from the North of England; for those who know, those from the North of England have a particular way of pronouncing vowels, especially the letter 'u'. It is not the same way that a Zulu person speaking English as their second language pronounces a 'u'. This now pointed out, it should become quickly apparent that the friendly assistant previously approached to help in my quest for nuts was having real difficulties in assisting. Eventually, abandoning any hope of actually understanding what I was asking her for, she took me on a detailed tour of the store, asking any other friendly assistants she came across if they knew where the 'nuts' were, pronounced in perfect Sheffield-ese. Of course, they had no idea either.

In desperation, as I had already traversed each aisle unsuccessfully on my own, I started adding prefixes to the offending noun. I tried 'hazelnuts', with little response. Only when I opted for 'peanuts' did I get an exclamation of delight as my friendly assistant finally figured out what I needed assistance with, and took me straight to their hiding place.

Exhausted from the encounter, I shuffled over to the moving conveyor belt at the checkout, dumped my nuts and other goods on its gently rolling surface, paid for them, then tottered home for a well-deserved cup of tea.

Translation from English to English continued to perplex for many years. It is quite isolating to realise that even a call to Directory Enquiries in search of a phone number is going to be a trial of endurance, as the Directory attempts to understand the Enquirer and vice versa.

Perhaps the pinnacle of achievement, however, was when, on a return trip to the UK, the lady at the counter in Boots couldn't understand what I was asking and needed Craig to explain ...

Language

This place is strange to me

    And I, it seems, am strange to you.

I thought my words the same as yours

    That language still made sense

Yet here I am an alien

    in this different land.

        Which land, to you, is home.

I've crossed a sea

    and a continent

But somehow thought I'd moved

    next door, to my neighbour's town

        whose customs I still knew.

So, with shock, I wake each day

    (Perhaps a little inward groan)

as once again I venture out

    in efforts to fit in.

To understand

    Be understood

Not just to look the same

but try to sound

and listen

like one of you, foreigners to me.

But I, the foreigner to you.

As time has passed my ear has tuned

to the frequency of you

A melody imbued with the note of my old

your new

A richer, clearer symphony

An orchestra complete.

Your song integral to the opera of me

And mine, I hope, of you.

Prayer

Father, thank you that through Jesus I am connected to others, whether they are similar to me or not. Thank you that my life is richer because of the people I share it with. Help me to add color, texture and the life of Jesus wherever I go.

8

Sitting on a Hard Kitchen Chair

And he made from one man every nation of mankind to live on all the face of the earth, having determined allotted periods and the boundaries of their dwelling place...

Acts 17:26

THERE COMES A TIME WHEN the ex-pat has the dawning realisation that this isn't some long, drawn-out holiday from which a return home will eventually result; rather, this is long-term life, a new normal, a new 'home'.

Well, at least for this ex-pat there was! Christmas with family had come and gone, braai etiquette was slowly being acquired and I'd finally figured out where the nuts were displayed in the supermarket. And now the hard work was really beginning.

In January 1998, I was granted Permanent Residency to stay in South Africa, the application for which had been quite a story in itself. Soon after arriving in Empangeni, I presented myself at the squat, red brick buildings of the always-heaving Department of Home Affairs in town. I plunged into the maelstrom of waiting locals, all waiting to register the happy occasions of birth or the sad realities of death, and everything in between.

I eventually found a sign for Permanent Residency applications and headed up the stairs in the direction it pointed. Here, it was considerably quieter, less busy with the noise of impatient people, more busy with the concentration of essential admin. I was shown into a lady's office, who asked to see all the documentation relevant to my application; this I duly handed over.

After some time checking through all the bits of paper, the lady, scrutinising my marriage certificate as she spoke, asked, 'So you were only married two weeks before leaving England for South Africa?'.

'Yes,' I meekly replied.

'Ah,' she countered. 'Before your residency can be granted, you may have to prove this wasn't a marriage of convenience, just so you could gain permanent living status in South Africa ...'.

I can still picture her behind her desk, the sweltering African sun streaming through the window off to her left as she glanced dubiously at my blue British passport. 'Probably not though,' she concluded.

A couple of months later, I received an A4 sheet of paper containing my new Permanent Residency status and number, no questions having been asked as to the convenience or otherwise of my marriage.

Permanent. The holiday was over.

One section of the residency form provides space for Occupation. Mine states I am a 'housewife'. I had no other job, no other form of daily employment, which I began to feel needed to change. (Incidentally, as a housewife, I did discover a great fruit and vegetable store in the nearby town of Richard's Bay, aptly named 'Housewives' Market'. Here I could replace the awful fresh produce found in all the supermarkets with some great seasonal offerings. Years later I was to discover that the store was owned by the in-laws of a friend I made through the pre-primary school Caragh and Leal attended as 'littlies' here in Durban!).

To return to my search for meaningful employment. This was hard to do for an English girl in a region where knowledge of Afrikaans was a basic requirement. And it wasn't simply language that was a barrier; history was against me.

Let me explain. A few weeks after settling into our new home, the wife of Craig's boss (he of the aforementioned potjie afternoon) invited me to have tea with some of the other mill wives. She herself had been an English outsider in an Afrikaans community - making the linguistic mistake of providing a bucket of potato salad for a braai rather than the requested bowl of said salad - and so was keen to help me connect.

It was a little daunting, entering her lounge full of ladies I didn't know, all of whom were wives of much longer standing than myself, many chatting away to each other in a language I didn't understand. I grabbed the proffered cup of tea and stood awkwardly to one side.

Eventually, one of the ladies called me over, asking me to join her and her friend as they sat on a flowery chintz-covered sofa. I perched on a nearby chair, after being introduced to Poppy (as I ignorantly thought her name. Turns out it was Poppie, not referring to a red flower of remembrance at all, but rather a small doll). 'Poppy' and her friend said, 'Hi, pleased to meet you', and then proceeded to embark on an animated conversation in Afrikaans.

It finally dawned on them that I had no idea what they were chatting about and was, in fact, feeling somewhat excluded, so they readily switched to English, much to my relief. It was a short-lived relief. Poppy embarked on a reminiscence of her strict childhood spent in Pretoria, unable to wear shorts or play in the garden on a Sunday in case the Dominee (priest) came to visit. She concluded her sorry tale by stating that her father had left home during the Second World War in order to fight - to her chagrin, on the side of the British. Bitterly she exclaimed, 'That's what finally killed him. And I still hate the British'

I honestly don't think she saw me as one of those same 'hated British' as I sat in front of her (she invited me to her house for tea when I was leaving later that afternoon), with my heart sinking to the floor as I felt the hurt of generations and the weight of deeds long past. But it cut me deeply, regardless. I went home and sat on the bottom step of our stairs and cried my eyes out.

Yes, the holiday was over.

I tried a couple of self-employment options after this. Hilariously, I made and sold 'Toad in the Hole' takeaway lunches to the factory workers, setting up a table in the car park from which to offer my wares. Hot and hungry pan boilers, welders and others peered cautiously at the sausages and Yorkshire pudding as they lay smothered in thick brown gravy. Not a roaring success, it must be said! Shortly after that, I was given the opportunity to run the tuck shop at the private school in the village ('Had my prowess as a caterer already spread?' I wondered.). I had aspirations of becoming the next big thing in lunchtime sandwich making and delivery, offering my by-now renowned specialties to all around - the quarry over the road, the offices in town. 'The Lunchbox' turned out to be a whole lot of work for not a lot of reward!

Early during this time, I discovered 'The Weekly Telegraph', a newspaper printed and distributed once a week and containing a round-up of news, both English and more international. I devoured this more-or-less from cover to cover, though of course skipping the mind-numbingly boring sports pages at the back. My favourite bit was a short section about ex-pat living, with stories sent in by British people living 'overseas'. It was often very funny, as they recounted the mishaps and adventures encountered as they settled into their new homes; it was also honest, describing how difficult it can be to join in and assimilate when seeking to adapt to another culture.

And I got to thinking, 'If I had to write about learning to settle in South Africa, and the differences between here and there, what would I say?'. I was reminded of a description Dad uses about restaurants - there are those where the sauce bottle is hidden behind the counter and only brought out when requested; there are those where the sauce bottle is a permanent fixture on the table; and there are those, at the bottom end of the scale, with a smashed sauce bottle on the table! Obviously, I couldn't use the analogy of a restaurant to describe a whole life, but I did think of something similar; living in England had been like relaxing in a comfy, well-plumped armchair, a cup of tea and a good book ready to hand.

South Africa, in contrast, was somewhat akin to sitting upright on a hard kitchen chair; it was at least a chair, rather than a distinctly less appealing cold floor, but it was still a hard, utilitarian, somewhat 'unpretty', chair.

Over the years, I've grown more accustomed to the seat on which I sit. I've been moulded and changed so it no longer feels uncomfortable; I've added a cushion or two of my own to soften some of the edges. Sitting 'upright' has undoubtedly been good for me - I have a firmer posture, greater resilience to difficulty or discomfort, wider eyes to see a different beauty and, at times, a harsher reality. Its only on those times when we take a break and return to the once-familiar armchair that is England that I am caught a little off guard.

But that's for next time ...

Prayer

Thank you, Father, that you have chosen every place I should live and for what period of time. Thank you that you have a reason for me being where I am at this particular time. Help me to seek you and so be able to fulfil all that you have planned and purposed.

9

South Africans Don't Lock Toilet Doors

The boundary lines have fallen for me in pleasant places; surely I have a delightful inheritance.

Psalms 16:6

SO HERE WE ARE AGAIN, another year of life in South Africa. As my time living away from the UK lengthens, the memories of difference become increasingly dimmed and how I live now seems as though it's how I've always done so.

That is until I take a visit back 'home'. As we did for Christmas 2018. Perhaps it was that we visited at a time when opposites are most apparent - anyone leaving Durban on a humid summer's evening in December who arrives at Heathrow on a crisp and cold winter's morning just the next day will know what I mean - but this trip reminded me, perhaps more than any other, of some of the smaller details which I'd completely forgotten about.

After collecting our bags from the ever-turning carousel, we loaded up our trolleys and headed out to catch the bus to the hire car pick up point. On first exiting the terminal, the initial nip of chilled, sunny air feels quite invigorating. After all, it wasn't too early in the day, perhaps just after 11 am, so we'd missed the worst of the iciness. By the time we'd stood around waiting for a larger car than the one we'd ordered to be located, invigoration had become blue lips, frozen fingers, and survivalist desperation.

Eventually, we were cosily ensconced in our Citroen Picasso, heater blasting, and on the road to Oxford. We decided we needed a quick pit stop for hot coffees and chocolate, as well as a timely dash to the loo, so we pulled over at the first services we could find. By now, we had ditched our hats, coats, scarves, and gloves, the sun was pouring through the windows and we were warm. And then we opened the doors.

I don't think I've ever seen Leal pull a coat on so quickly.

On previous visits, when we've stopped for coffee in one of the various franchise stores that abound in shopping malls and service stations, Caragh and Leal have bemoaned the inexplicable absence of sumptuous thick milkshakes. Not so this time - the hotter the chocolate the better.

All too quickly we were finished and heading back into the sub-Arctic temperatures of midday in December in England.

"Fires, fairy lights, and festivities

So started our just-over-two-week visit to the UK at Christmas. And with it, various small reminders of what made transitioning between my old and new homes at times challenging, bewildering or just downright amusing.

To start with, home design and comforts. When I landed in South Africa on 4th July 1997 and disappeared into the softening sunset of a winter afternoon, I was little prepared for the tiled, uncarpeted floors, loose-fitting doors and windows and complete lack of any sort of central heating system. In fact, heat sources, in general, seemed to be in short supply! I spent much of those first few months feeling frozen cold, wearing whatever jerseys and jackets I'd brought with me, and being constantly told that, as I was from England, I should be used to it.

Used to being cold outside, maybe. To being even colder inside, definitely not (in fact, as I sit here writing, the sun is shining in gentle warmth outside, but my fingers can hardly type, it's so cold inside the house!).

Not only were there no fires roaring in family grates, neither were there fairy lights and candles twinkling and flickering in every window and on every surface. Winter, in my experience, had always been a cosy, warmly-lit affair, early darkness punctuated with oases of soft yellow light, pools of delicate white. It hadn't really been the bright glare of a fluorescent kitchen strip or centrally hanging, barely shaded light bulb as it was in our first marital home.

Arriving at my sister's new house last December, I felt the warm embrace of home. She has a passion for fairy lights that exceeds my own, her heating is gloriously efficient and there wasn't a strip light to be seen.

Of course, I have since Anglicised my own winter living here in Umdloti. I have solar powered fairy lights entwined in trees in the garden, all of which light up magically as 'on' buttons are pressed by the stealthy fingers of a darkening evening; I have a new wood-burning stove in the lounge that emits a furnace-like warmth (and is also very good at cooking jacket pototoes...) and I have a surfeit of dim lamps and light fixtures, so much so that even the sharpest of young eyes find reading in the evening a little stretching!

"Rules of the road

After spending time in the city of the Dark Blues, we headed on over to Cambridge, home of the Light crew. And here I received another reminder of one of those little quirks of difference.

We were due to stay in a rented cottage, right in the centre of Cambridge. And we had a reasonably large hire car. For those who know Cambridge well, these do not a happy combination make. I think the road of our home was possibly one of the narrowest there may be, and of course, being in the centre, empty parking spaces were non-existent.

As we shunted our way into a space more suited to a bicycle, I started to take notice of the company around us; cars jammed in every possible gap and space, all facing whatever direction they happened to be driving in when they'd been brought to their final destinations. And then I realised why this seemed so strange, so out of place.

It wasn't the narrowness of the road, where now I see wide expanses of tarmac or concrete in most places that I drive and park; it wasn't the clouds of cold breath misting the windows as we strained into place. It was the haphazard, disorganised nature of the parking that struck me.

For here, in the land of freedom from the constraint of following rules and orders, parking is the one area of public life that is remarkably disciplined.

Craig did much of the driving when we first lived in Empangeni, mainly because we only had one car so I couldn't nip out and about when I felt like it. On one of the early occasions when I did drive, we went to visit friends in town.

In SA, we drive on the left-hand side of the road, as in the UK. So that wasn't something I had to conquer. However, as we drew up to our friend's house, which happened to be over on the right, I pulled across the road to park beside their gate. I was off the road, but of course now facing any oncoming traffic. Thinking nothing of this, I started to climb out of the car when Craig called me back. 'You can't park like this', he told me. Turns out that you can't just park willy-nilly on South African streets like you can in England; you have to be parked in the same direction as the traffic flow.

Back in the car I climbed and turned around...

"And so to those toilet doors!

After a great few days catching up with favourite sights and old friends, we left Cambridge and went to spend Christmas week with my folks in Cornwall.

My folks' home was pretty full with all our comings and goings. My sister and family were staying (seven of them in total), plus us four and of course the hosts, Mum and Dad, themselves. We had a wonderful time eating, playing, chatting and resting.

And of course, we utilised all available ablutions. As an aside, that's a word I never, ever used until I came to South Africa. On our first camping trip, the 'ablutions' were helpfully pointed out to me, as we passed what I knew as the toilet and shower block. And so the name has stuck, despite feeling as though I have been transported to a 1920's Boarding School for Young Ladies!

Anyway, to return to Cornwall. At my folks home, there is a guest toilet just inside the front door, at the bottom of the stairs next to the Coats' Cupboard. On one occasion, I desired to visit said small room, only to discover it locked.

Locked! Memories came flooding back. Nerve-wracking moments spent trying to find keys or bolts to lock myself in whilst performing the most private of duties. I soon worked out that a closed door in South Africa is the same as a locked one in England; an open door means it's free. A door into such a space in the UK is always closed, regardless of its occupancy. This unspoken understanding means that a key is never needed, a bolt unnecessary. And when really not sure - a quick knock will suffice.

Of course, now when in the UK, I have the opposite concern - I completely forget to lock the door and therefore experience panic that I may not remain undisturbed for the duration of my stay...

*"**The joy of contrary living**

I've found its sometimes these small, seemingly-insignificant oddities that take the longest to become accustomed to, perhaps because they are barely noticed by those who perform them and yet they highlight the 'other-ness' of someone not long initiated into them.

And yet, almost because of the minutiae of life that they represent, these quirks and habits, when embraced and combined with the habits of another place, enlarge the experience in both places I call home. A plastic washing up bowl, for example, is a rare sight in a South African kitchen, as compared to where I grew up. It took me an age to get used to filling one side of a stainless steel double sink. And then drought hit the region, and suddenly a method of retaining the washing water for re-use in the garden became a necessity, and my grey plastic bowl was purchased for the purpose. An unconscious habit from one place made deliberate use of in the other.

I will never become a South African. At heart, I will always be the English girl I was born as. But, over time, as I add layers of new to the foundations of old I become more than I would ever have been if I'd remained in just one place, among just one people. Friends who visit comment on my fairy lights and fireplace, enjoying a little touch of something unfamiliar in my home. A little bit of England perhaps. And I now park in the direction of travel, regardless of whether I am in the southern or northern hemispheres. A touch of South African civility maybe.

And hopefully, I'll remember where to lock the toilet door.

Prayer

Thank you, Father, that you have placed me in both a safe and pleasant place, and that you have made my boundaries secure. Help me to be content in any and every circumstance as I trust in your love and provision.

I'm a British ex-pat who has lived in South Africa for a little over twenty years. My husband and I live with our two teenage children on the east coast, a few miles north of the city of Durban. We overlook the Indian Ocean where we have the privilege of watching dolphins and whales at play.

My first book 'The Outskirts of His Glory' was published in May 2019. The book is a Christian devotional and poetry collection exploring the many surprising ways that God can speak to us through His creation. I have drawn on my travels in and around South Africa, as well as further afield, to hopefully inspire each of us to slow down and perhaps listen more carefully to the 'whispers of His ways' (Job 26:14) that are all around us.

Since publishing 'Outskirts' I have had the privilege of speaking at a number of local churches and even have a weekly slot on a Christian radio station. I have also continued writing by contributing to a variety of blogs and online writing communities as well as developing my own website and blog.

Want to know more? You can find me at

Website: www.annajensen.co.uk

Facebook: https://www.facebook.com/annaloujensen

Instagram: https://www.instagram.com/annaloujens/

Twitter: https://twitter.com/annalouj

I send out a (more-or-less monthly) newsletter which you can subscribe to if you'd like to find out what's happening in the world of Anna! It includes my latest blog post about whatever God is saying and doing in my life at any given moment. There's also book reviews, guest posts and promos. Oh, and it's free and you can unsubscribe whenever you like.

I'd love to hear from you too. You can email me at hello@annajensen.co.za

More from Anna

If you enjoyed this devotional from Anna, you might like to check out her other books. Click on the image to go the Amazon sales pages, or you buy direct from Anna's website www.annajensen.co.uk

The Outskirts of His Glory

Join Anna Jensen and her family as they travel to seek out and experience the odd and unexpected of God's creation.

Poetry and Prayer

'I started writing poems in earnest just a few years ago...My poetry will always begin and end with Jesus. He is the master craftsman, the great author, The Word. In this way, each poem is indeed a prayer; of thanksgiving, of worship, of truth whispered in innermost parts. As you read both the poems and the thinking behind them, I pray that Jesus would woo you afresh by his presence.'